Freshwater PREDATORS

Craig Allen

Badger Publishing Limited
Oldmedow Road,
Hardwick Industrial Estate,
King's Lynn PE30 4JJ
Telephone: 01438 791037

www.badgerlearning.co.uk

2 4 6 8 10 9 7 5 3

Freshwater Predators ISBN 978-1-78147-547-8

Publisher: Susan Ross
Senior Editor: Danny Pearson
Designer: Fiona Grant

Photos: Cover image: REX/Charles Hotham/SplashdownDirect
Page 4: Barcroft Media/Getty Images
Page 5: Jean-Michel Labat/ardea
Page 6: Morales/age fotostock/Getty Images
Page 7: Juan Manuel Borrer/Biosphoto/FLP
Page 8: Alex Mustard/naturepl
Page 9: Zac Macaulay/Photographer's Choice/Getty Images
Page 10: B Barker/Newspix/REX
Page 11: Justin Lewis/cultura/Corbis
Page 12: AlamyCelebrity/Alamy
Page 13: AlamyCelebrity/Alamy
Page 14: Robert F.Sisson/National Geographic/Getty Images
Page 15: Oxford Scientific/Getty Images
Page 16: Tom Stack/Alamy
Page 17: George Grail/National Geographic/Getty Images
Page 18: Hermann Brehm/naturepl
Page 19: Andre Seale/Alamy
Page 21: Solent News/REX
Page 22: Apichart Weerawong/AP/Press Association Images
Page 23: REX/Bournemouth News
Page 25: REX/Andy Rouse
Page 26: DENIS-HUOT/ Getty Images
Page 28: Rex/outtherefilms
Page 29: Pat Morris/ardea
Page 30: Stock Connection/REX
Page 31: Ueslei Marcelino/Reuters/Corbis

Attempts to contact all copyright holders have been made.
If any omitted would care to contact Badger Learning, we will be happy to make appropriate arrangements.

Contents

1. Anaconda

The anaconda is one of the largest snakes on the planet. It can grow to an incredible 9 metres long and can weigh up to 250 kilograms.

Anacondas are found in many countries in South America. They live in rivers and swamps and can stay under water for up to ten minutes at a time before coming up to breathe.

Some snakes kill their prey by injecting venom through a bite – but not the anaconda. The anaconda is a member of the constrictor family. When it attacks, it springs from the water and grabs hold of its prey. Then the anaconda wraps its body around its prey and squeezes hard until it stops breathing.

The anaconda then eats its prey whole!

It can take months for the anaconda to digest its prey. All animals can find themselves on the menu of this monstrous predator. Not even small crocodiles are safe.

WOW! facts

Anacondas mainly hunt at night (nocturnal) and prefer to hunt in water but they can also hunt by day and on land if they need to.

Danger level to humans 7

2. Bull shark

Bull sharks – but don't they live in salt water?

Yes, correct, but one fact that you might not know is that they can also survive in fresh water!

Bull sharks are among the most aggressive sharks in salt water. However, now they have found alternative homes in fresh water, they are certainly a predator to be both respected and feared.

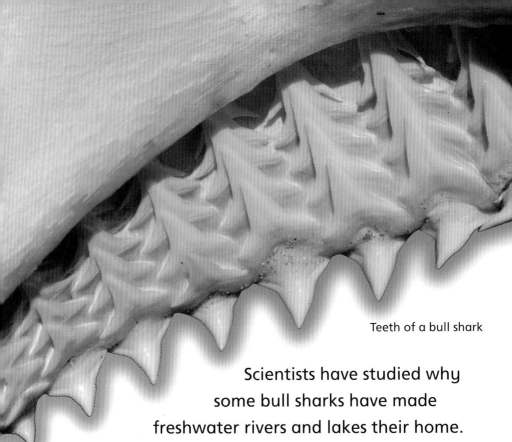
Teeth of a bull shark

Scientists have studied why
some bull sharks have made
freshwater rivers and lakes their home.
It is believed that large lakes are a safe place
for them to breed and raise their young.

With a huge abundance of food, bull sharks can
easily survive in the freshwater habitats of Australia
and America.

The bull shark survives in fresh water by storing salt
and using it slowly. This unique process allows the
shark to move in and out of freshwater river systems
as and when it pleases.

Bull sharks can grow to over 3 metres in length and weigh a staggering 230 kilograms.

WOW! facts

The film *Jaws* was originally inspired by a bull shark attack in America – yes, in a freshwater lake!

Danger level to humans 9

3. Diving bell spider

The diving bell spider is a truly remarkable freshwater predator and is unique among spiders.

When you think of a spider, it is out of water. Right? Well, not this one…

The diving bell spider is the only spider in the world to spend its life under water.

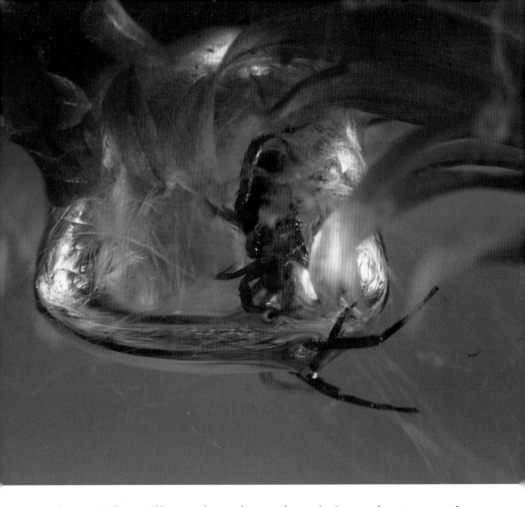

This spider still needs to breathe air in order to survive – so how does it do it?

First, it spins a dome-shaped web between two plants under water. It then uses the hair on its legs to trap air in when it travels to the surface. Next, the diving bell spider travels back down to the dome. It releases the trapped air from its legs into the dome.

Like other spiders, the diving bell spider eats flies and insects. It traps its prey in the dome-shaped web. Just like an ordinary land spider, its web is sticky. So when prey comes into contact with it, it gets stuck, leaving the diving bell spider free to feed.

These spiders can be found across Europe as well as in parts of Asia. It lives in small ponds and streams.

WOW! facts

In most other species of spider, the female is larger than the male. But with the diving bell spider the male is bigger.

Danger level to humans 0

4. Electric eel

The electric eel is without a doubt one of the weirdest looking freshwater predators on the planet.

Found in many rivers in South America, the electric eel can cause serious damage to any living creature that gets in its way.

This is because the electric eel has the ability to generate 500 volts of electricity from its body!

When the eel releases electricity into the water, all the surrounding animals become stunned – some more than others, depending on their size. The electric eel can then pick off its prey more easily.

Although electric eels live in fresh water, they can also be found on land. That's because the electric eel is an air-breather and can survive out of water with ease. When in water, the electric eel must surface every ten minutes to inhale oxygen to breathe. If it doesn't, it will die.

With some electric eels reaching over 2.5 metres in length and weighing over 18kg, this is one predator not to be messed with!

Electric eels have been accused of causing deaths in humans across South America. While the electrical charge given off by one electric eel is not enough to stun a human, the charge from many combined together is.

If this was to happen, a human could easily drown.

Danger level to humans 7

5. Giant freshwater stingray

The giant freshwater stingray is one of the most powerful predators lurking in fresh water. It is also one of the world's largest freshwater predatory fish.

The giant freshwater stingray can grow to over 4.8 metres in length and can weigh more than 450 kilograms!

These stingrays lie at the bottom of rivers waiting for their prey to come to them. Giant stingrays are slower than other predators so they save their energy and wait until the right time to strike.

Giant stingrays can be found in northern Australia, Borneo, New Guinea and Thailand.

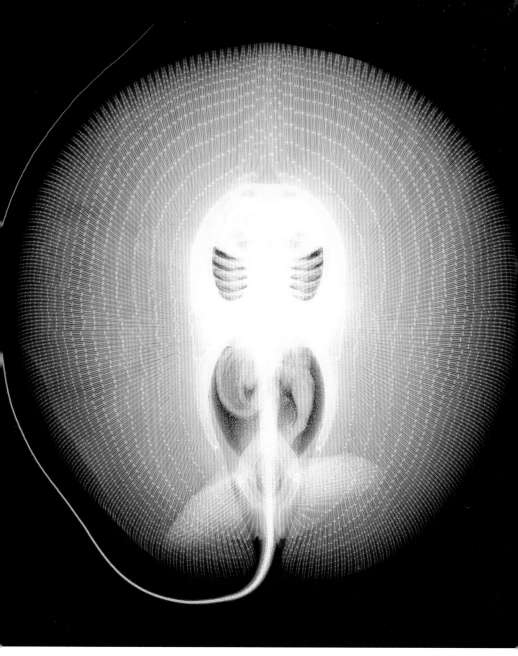

X-ray of a stingray

Fishermen from all around the world travel to these destinations with the hope of catching this formidable predator. Unfortunately, they often find it to be a great challenge.

The giant freshwater stingray has an impressive tail. This tail can be used for self-defence, if needed. On the end of the tail is a large spike, which can cause serious damage to anything that gets in its way.

This stinger can be as long as 38 centimetres and, if it comes into contact with an unlucky victim, it can transfer toxins into the wound causing major discomfort.

WOW! facts

Large stingrays have been known to pull boats for over a mile when a fisherman has hooked one of these creatures.

Danger level to humans 7

6. Nile crocodile

Unlike many other freshwater predators, Nile crocodiles are extremely dangerous to humans. They eat meat – and what are we made from? You guessed it, meat!

Nile crocodiles can be found in many parts of Africa, including the River Nile, which is where it gets its name from.

It is estimated that Nile crocodiles are responsible for around 200 human deaths per year, although it may be more. Many people have simply vanished from the water's edge, never to be seen again.

The Nile crocodile kills more humans per year than bears, lions and sharks put together!

In the wild, the Nile crocodile can weigh up to 225kg and grow up to an unbelievable 6 metres in length!

The Nile crocodile usually eats any fish it can find in its natural habitat, like the Nile perch, another huge freshwater predator. However, if a human was to get in the way then its killer instinct would take over.

The Nile crocodile is a more effective predator in water but land animals are also on the menu. Anything made of meat is a potential target and with the Nile crocodile being able to eat up to half its own body weight in a day, all creatures great and small must watch out!

People living alongside the River Nile have built barricades by the side of the water. These prevent the crocodiles from going into that area, so the people are able to collect water without fear of being attacked.

Danger level to humans 10

7. Vampire fish

The real name for the vampire fish is the Payara. It was given the name 'vampire fish' for obvious reasons.

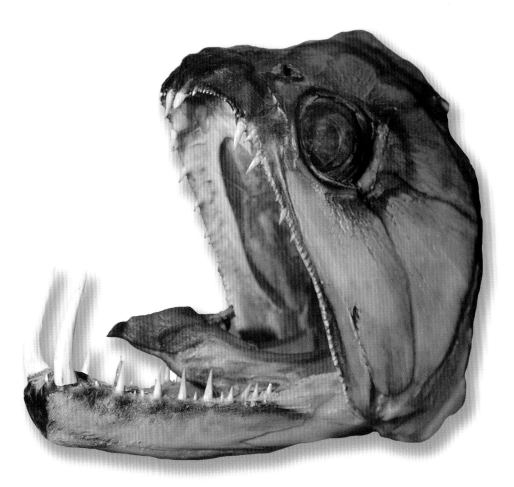

Vampire fish have many razor-sharp teeth but the two huge fangs at the front are more deadly and are used when hunting. The fangs fit into nasal pockets located on the top of the fish's head so it does not get hurt when it closes its mouth.

The vampire fish is one of the fastest predators in the Amazon River. Once it locates and attacks its prey, there is no stopping it.

This fish attacks and maims its prey by using the two fangs to impale it. The vampire fish will attack any fish up to a third of its own body size.

It can be found in many countries in South America and throughout the Amazon River.

Some very large vampire fish weighing over 18kg have been found in Bolivia, Brazil, Colombia and Venezuela.

Just like many other freshwater predators, the vampire fish likes to hunt in fast-flowing waters. There are many fast-flowing rapids located throughout the Amazon River.

WOW! facts

When the vampire fish is ready to eat its prey, it swallows the fish whole, head first. The unlucky victim is often still alive but too wounded to make an escape.

Danger level to humans 5

Index